THE BOOK
OF MY HEALING

This journal belongs to:

———————————————————————

Born on:

———————————————————————

In this place:

———————————————————————

I began this journal on:

———————————————————————

I would like to pass this journal on to:

———————————————————————

THE BOOK OF MY HEALING

A Journal of Your Recovery in 150 Questions

Peggy Schmidt

Concept by David Marshall

HYPERION

NEW YORK

Copyright © 2000 Peggy Schmidt

All rights reserved. No part of this book may be used or
reproduced in any manner whatsoever without the written permission
of the Publisher. Printed in the United States of America.
For information address Hyperion, 77 West 66th Street,
New York, New York, 10023-6298.

Book design by Ruth Lee

ISBN: 0-7868-6613-6

First Edition

1 3 5 7 9 10 8 6 4 2

To

Robert Allen Schmidt
1957–1995

Contents

Why Keep a Journal?

The palest ink is better than the best memory.
—Chinese proverb

The idea for this book took shape one night as I lay in bed unable to sleep because of the pain of several broken ribs and a bruised kidney—the result of a horseback-riding accident. While my injuries were not life-threatening and healed within a few months, I did some of the same soul-searching that those who experience a serious accident or illness confront.

- You wonder "Why me?"
- You worry about how people who depend on you will get through the coming weeks, months, or even years without the help or support you were until recently able to provide.
- You reluctantly realize that you may have to depend on others, or even worse, ask others for help in getting through each day.

- You put your trust in medical experts who have so much control over your health and the quality of your life.
- You reflect on your future well-being and your mortality, and wonder if life will ever quite be the same again.
- You think about dying, perhaps for the first time in your life.

Just as important in shaping this book, however, was the three-year illness of a friend. Vivien was diagnosed with cervical cancer at the age of fifty. I got to know her much better during the time she was ill because she was able to share her inner thoughts with others in a way she never had before. She talked about the new emotional terrain she was encountering. She spoke articulately about her experiences with the health care establishment, the many choices she faced as her cancer spread, and how her illness changed her view of life. Friends of mine often remarked, "It must be so depressing to spend time with her," particularly as her disease progressed. But quite the opposite was true: It was uplifting to be with her because she was willing to share her perspective as someone who was facing an interrupted life.

It was not until my own accident that I thought how wonderful it would have been had she committed her thoughts to writing, so that those of us who were so touched by her courage and optimism could have read them whenever we needed inspiration.

This journal is for you if you are experiencing or have already gone through a serious illness or accident. Or you may have a chronic illness that is characterized by periods of functioning well and, at other times, being too sick to get out of bed. The road to healing, whether it involves healing of the body or the spirit, or both, is an emotional roller-coaster and often a life-changing journey.

Putting your thoughts and feelings into words is a way of externalizing what you are going through. Professional writers often say they write of their pain and joy because it is a way of making sense of deeply felt emotions. Writing provides a way to get through bad times and celebrate good times. Or, as author and dramatist David Hare writes, "The act of writing is the act of discovering what you believe."

Injury and disease are as much intrusions on your psychological well-being as they are your health. When either becomes a part of your life for the short- or long-term, writing about your experience can help you gain a perspective you might not otherwise have. And it may help you end grieving over your loss and move forward.

The way this journal is organized can also help you see how far you've come with your healing. It starts with recollections of the early days of the diagnosis of your illness or the event of your accident and follows through the stages of coping—physically, emotionally, and spiritually. It's easy to lose sight of progress made and insights achieved if they're not expressed in words. Completing this journal can help you see the milestones that are etched into this period of your life.

While the journal is meant to be a record for your own reflection, it can also be shared with loved ones. It's often hard to tell family and friends how you really feel—how pain, surgery, medication, or uncertainty interferes with you being yourself. It may be difficult, too, to express in conversation how much their words and gestures of support mean to you. Letting those who care about you read your thoughts can give them insights they may not otherwise have.

Research Says Writing Promotes Healing

Perhaps the best reason for writing in this journal is that expressing your feelings and thoughts in writing may result in improved health. In 1999, the *Journal of the American Medical Association* published the first study findings demonstrating that writing about past stressful life experiences decreased the symptoms of some patients with asthma or rheumatoid arthritis. "Ventilation of negative emotion, even just to an unknown reader, seems to have helped these patients acknowledge, bear, and put into perspective their distress," wrote David Spiegel, MD, a psychiatrist at Stanford University School of Medicine, in an editorial that accompanied the study.

Joshua Smyth, MD, one of the principal researchers of the study, used the techniques developed by James W. Pennebaker, PhD, a psychologist who has studied the effects of structured writing on mental and physical health for sixteen years. Participants in studies are asked to write about the most stressful event in their lives for twenty minutes a day for three consecutive days. About half of the patients in Dr. Smyth's study showed clinically measured signs of improved health up to four months after the writing exercise.

Why does writing, particularly about personal trauma, have a positive effect on health? "We all carry around issues, conflicts, or secrets that are difficult to talk to others about," explains Pennebaker, author of *Opening Up: The Healing Power of Expressing Emotions* (Guilford Press). "Writing about something that bothers us helps us come to terms even with events we don't fully understand, and then we can go on with other things."

In a study he conducted with researcher Sandy Beal, Pennebaker found that healthy subjects who were asked to write about a traumatic event in their lives and how they felt about it showed improved immune system functioning six weeks after the three-day writing experiment.

As a result of his work, Pennebaker has come up with several guidelines that help increase the potential of using writing as a tool for healing.

• Write about your feelings, not just facts or events. It's critical to give voice to your emotions if you want to experience a positive outcome. It's fine to include details about the chronology of what happened or to describe things you observed, but you must also write about how those things made you feel and why. The more reflective your writing, the more beneficial it will be as a tool in healing.

- Write without worrying about the mechanics of writing. Don't concern yourself with sentence structure or length, spelling, or even the tone of your work. It's far more important to get your reactions and thoughts down on paper.
- Write for yourself. You are more likely to write candidly and without restraint if you write with the idea that you are the only one who will be reading your words.
- Try a ten-minute warm-up period. If the idea of starting seems too daunting, try writing about easy topics—even what your plans are for the day—for a short period before you begin writing about a more difficult subject.
- Write when it works for you, in a space that is comfortable and free of distractions. Pennebaker found that a "unique setting" seemed to help people write more easily. If you're mobile, you may want to consider going to a place such as a public library.
- Tape yourself if you don't want to write or have difficulty writing.

How might writing about illness-related issues benefit you? "When you become seriously ill through disease or an accident, family members or friends may not be able to share their feelings with you or listen to yours," says Pennebaker. "To cope with what's going on, they pretend that everything is going to be all right, when both of you know that your life may never be the same as it once was. Writing can be an outlet to express what you're going through and how you feel, and that can help put things in perspective."

Researchers do not yet understand why writing about emotions boosts immunological functioning or how long the effects last. But using writing as a strategy for healing costs nothing, is relatively easy to do, and holds the promise of enabling one to make the emotional journey through an illness with more confidence and peace of mind.

How to Use This Book

The form of this book asks for your handwritten thoughts. Questions are presented in groups so that you can choose to answer those that best describe your situation.

If writing is too fatiguing or difficult for you, you may be able to dictate entries to a friend or family member who agrees to be your scribe. In fact, it can be a special way to share time together, particularly if you're in a hospital or care facility. Another option: use a tape recorder to answer the questions. Save transcribing for a time when you're feeling stronger, or ask a friend to do that for you.

You need not fill out the journal in the order the questions are presented. Neither is it critical that you fill out the journal as things happen—at times, you may not have the strength or mental clarity to put your thoughts in writing. Once you do have the strength and presence of mind to write, it's a good idea to start your journal so that your thoughts, experiences, and emotions are still fresh in your mind. Finally, not every question or question cluster will fit your situation, so you can substitute your own question or use the space to expand on your answer to the previous question.

Section I
Life Interrupted

Diagnosis

- My illness or accident happened this way . . .
- The diagnosis of medical professionals was . . .
- This is how long it took for my illness to be diagnosed . . .
- I knew something was wrong because of these symptoms . . .
- I would describe my pain this way . . .
- What is not known about my prognosis at this time is . . .

I understand now that sickness makes no appointment and is not impressed with busy lives or concerned with interrupting them.

—*Writer Faye Moscowitz*

*D*on't defy the diagnosis, try to defy the verdict.
— *Author Norman Cousins*

_____

_____

_____

_____

_____

_____

_____

_____

_____

_____

We must travel in the direction of our fear.
—*Author and poet John Berryman*

God grant me the serenity
To accept the things I cannot change
Courage to change things I can
And wisdom to know the difference.

—Religious and social thinker
Reinhold Niebuhr

_____

_____

_____

_____

_____

_____

_____

_____

_____

Reaction

- My initial reaction was . . .
- I was able to acknowledge the seriousness of my illness or injury (from the beginning, after these tests, after consulting with these medical professionals) . . .
- I shared the news of what happened to me (when, how, and with whom) . . .
- What I was/am most reluctant to tell my friends and family was/is . . .
- Their reactions were . . .
- The hardest part of trying to put on a brave front or to act normal is . . .

*B*e willing to have it so; acceptance of what has happened is the first step to overcoming the consequences of any misfortune.

—*Philosopher William James*

*W*hat seem to us bitter trials are often blessings in disguise.
—*Poet, playwright, and novelist Oscar Wilde*

A single event can awaken within us a stranger totally unknown to us. To live is to be slowly born.

—*Novelist, essayist, and aviator*
Antoine de Saint-Exupéry

*D*ecisions

- My biggest frustration about what I know or don't know about my illness or injuries at this time is . . .
- I found these sources (books, articles, websites) to be most useful . . .
- I talked to these people, who shared their expertise or experience . . .
- The friends and relatives who have been most useful in helping me find information and making choices were . . .
- The time I spent trying to come to a decision has been characterized by . . .

_____

_____

_____

_____

_____

_____

_____

*E*very wall is a door.
—*Poet, essayist, and philosopher*
Ralph Waldo Emerson

*P*essimism operates in a narrowed field of vision that fails to take into account the possibilities at the outer edges of experience.

—*Author Norman Cousins*

*D*o what you can, with what you have, where you are.

—*President Theodore Roosevelt*

_____

_____

_____

_____

_____

_____

_____

_____

_____

_____

The ultimate measure of a man is not where he
stands in moments of comfort and convenience,
but where he stands at times of challenge and
controversy.

> —*Civil rights leader*
> *Rev. Martin Luther King, Jr.*

*O*ur very infirmities help us unexpectedly.
—*Philosopher William James*

Reflections on
My Medical Care

$\mathcal{T}$reatment

- The most difficult aspect of going ahead with treatment or care was . . .
- I put off (surgery, taking medication, undergoing treatment) until . . .
- The kind of treatment I opted for was:
- It involves . . .
- The risks are . . .
- The best outcome would be . . .
- My fears and hopes about undergoing treatment included . . .

_____

_____

_____

_____

_____

_____

_____

*U*nhurt people are not much good in the world.
—*Author Enid Starkie*

*W*hen things come to the worst, they generally mend.

—*Poet and novelist Susanna Moodie*

_____

_____

_____

_____

_____

_____

_____

_____

_____

*T*he desire to take medicine is perhaps the greatest feature which distinguishes man from animals.

—Physician William Osler

$\mathcal{R}$eaction

- Here's what I remember most about the early stages of my treatment . . .
- My physical reactions to medication/treatment included . . .
- Over time, my reaction to medication/treatment changed in these ways . . .
- There were times when I felt discouraged about continuing treatment because . . .
- What encouraged me to stick with it was . . .
- I have been told that treatment options for my illness won't cure me, but may alleviate symptoms or delay the onset of more debilitating conditions. Given that scenario, my feelings about undergoing treatment are . . .

*F*or every ailment under the sun
    There is a remedy, or there is none;
    If there be one, try to find it
    If there be none, never mind it.

                           —*Mother Goose*

*A*lthough the world is full of suffering, it is full also of the overcoming of it.

—*Memoirist, essayist, and lecturer Helen Keller*

Hospitalization

- What I found most difficult/interesting about being in the hospital was:
- Here's what I learned from listening to and observing other hospital patients:
- What I most liked/disliked about having roommates was:
- Here's what I wish I could have said to well-meaning visitors whom I found intrusive or inconsiderate . . .
- This is how I felt about being cared for:

Outpatient Care

- What was difficult about outpatient care for me or those who helped care for me was . . .
- The times when I feel so ill that I wish I could be cared for in a health care facility were (are) . . .
- Getting care on an outpatient basis helped me feel more independent and on the road to recovery because . . .

$\mathcal{M}$etaphorically and actually, illness and hospitalizations strip us of what covered and protected us in many ways. Indignities happen.
—*Writer and lecturer Jean Shinoda Bolen*

*N*othing is more essential in the treatment of serious disease than the liberation of the patient from panic and foreboding.

—*Author Norman Cousins*

*C*ompassion for myself is the most powerful healer of them all.

—Psychiatrist and author
Theodore Isaac Rubin

What saves a man is to take a step. Then another step. It is always the same step, but you have to take it.

—*Novelist, essayist, and aviator*
Antoine de Saint-Exupéry

Emotions

- I feel disassociated from my body when . . .
- The worst indignities that I have to endure as a patient are . . .
- When I pray or reflect on my situation, this is what is on my mind:
- My illness or injury changed how I thought about my body in this way:
- I was able to deal with what was happening to me physically by . . .

*T*o live life is so startling, it leaves little time for
anything else.

—*Poet Emily Dickinson*

Self-pity in its early stages is as snug as a feather mattress. Only when it hardens does it become uncomfortable.

—*Poet Maya Angelou*

*T*he secret of seeing is to sail on solar wind. Hone and spread your spirit, till you yourself are a sail, whetted, translucent, broadside to the merest puff.

—*Writer Annie Dillard*

Family & Friends

- I especially appreciate . . . for . . .
- I treasure these words of caring or support from . . .
- I enjoy visits/conversations with . . .
- I received unexpected support from . . .
- I am disappointed in the lack of support/friendship from . . .

Caregivers

- I am indebted to this person for caring for me, especially for these things:
- I do not feel comfortable depending on family and friends to take care of me, and wish I could relieve their burden by . . .
- Here is what I would like to be able to say to those who care for me:

_____

_____

_____

_____

_____

_____

I was sick, and ye visited me.

—*Matthew 25:36*

*W*ithout friends no one would choose to live,
though he had all other goods.
—*Philosopher Aristotle*

_____

_____

_____

_____

_____

_____

_____

_____

_____

_____

*H*ave no friends not equal to yourself.
—*Philosopher Confucius*

Health Care Professionals

- I'm glad I asked my doctors about (my prognosis, what kind of physical reactions to expect, my options) . . .
- I (am) was most afraid to ask my doctors about . . .
- What I wish I had known to ask doctors or wish my doctors had told me was . . .
- This is how I think the nursing staff would characterize me as a patient:
- I was touched and grateful for the help and caring of these medical professionals:
- What most upset me about how I was treated by medical professionals was . . .

*N*ature, time, and patience are the three great physicians.

—*Proverb*

*T*he human body experiences a powerful gravitational pull in the direction of hope. That is why the patient's hopes are the physician's secret weapon. They are the hidden ingredients in any prescription.

—*Author Norman Cousins*

I observe the physician with the same diligence as he the disease.

—*Poet John Donne*

*W*hen we honestly ask ourselves which person in our lives means the most to us, we often find it is those who . . . have chosen to share our pain and touch our wounds with a warm and tender hand.

—*Author Henri J.M. Nouwen*

Section 3
Self-Discovery

Seeing the World Anew

- When I left the hospital, I found a new thrill in these familiar objects or routines:
- When I was able to go out-of-doors for the first time, these are the sights, sounds, and textures I experienced in a new way:
- These things used to bother or upset me, but don't seem so important anymore:
- I have a new appreciation for . . .

*K*eep your face to the sunshine and you cannot
see the shadow.

—*Memoirist, essayist, and lecturer*
Helen Keller

$\mathcal{M}$y barn having burned to the ground, I can now see the moon.

—*Taoist saying*

*T*wo men looked out from prison bars
One saw mud, the other saw stars.

—*Unknown*

$\mathcal{E}$motions

- I find I am able to feel happy when . . .
- I find myself in tears when . . .
- I feel upset or frustrated when . . .
- I feel most able to laugh when . . .
- I experience loneliness in this way:

I hadn't planned to learn that one of the things that makes life worth living is the thought that whatever it is that happened, it could have been worse.
—*Novelist Jane Smiley*

*T*o bear is to conquer our fate.
—*Poet Thomas Campbell*

*P*ray that your loneliness may spur you into finding
something to live for, great enough to die for.
　　　　　—*United Nations Secretary-*
　　　　　　General Dag Hammarskjöld

_____

_____

_____

_____

_____

_____

_____

_____

_____

_____

_____

*I*nward *Journey*

- I realized that I had inner strength and determination that I never knew I had before. This recognition occurred when. . .
- In my darkest moments, I found strength to go on by . . .
- Beyond grieving the loss of my health, I also grieved over these things that had happened earlier in my life . . .
- I learned things about myself that I never knew before when. . .

The longest journey is the journey inward.
—*United Nations Secretary-*
General Dag Hammarskjöld

*O*ne doesn't discover new lands without consenting to lose sight of the shore for a very long time.
—*Novelist, critic, and essayist*
André Gide

*U*nless one says goodbye to what one loves, and unless one travels to completely new territories, one can expect merely a long wearing away of oneself.

—*Painter, printmaker, and sculptor Jean Dubuffet*

*G*etting *Better*

- What made me decide to do everything in my power to recover to the fullest extent possible was . . .
- What was most difficult about the transition to caring for myself was . . .
- I believe I will make it through my illness or injury more successfully because of these personal qualities . . .
- I found myself able to heal more quickly because of these things that I did for others . . .

For those whose injuries are permanently disabling, or for those with a chronic illness:

- I want to believe that my life will be worth living, but these are the doubts that I secretly harbor . . .
- It took time for me to accept things I could no longer do easily or by myself, but I was slowly able to come to grips with that realization by . . .
- I do not want to be thought of or treated as a sick person, so I (continue working part-time, keep up with these activities, try to do these things for myself) . . .
- I realize that there will always be limitations on what I will be able to do, but I feel I can handle that because . . .

*T*he days come and go like muffled and veiled figures sent from a distant friendly party, but they say nothing, and if we do not use the gifts they bring, they carry them as silently away.

—*Poet, essayist, and philosopher*
Ralph Waldo Emerson

*Y*ou may not have a choice about what is happening to your body, but you do have a choice about what is happening to your mind.

—*Teacher Kathy Hoekenga*

*G*rowth demands a temporary surrender of security.

—*Writer Gail Sheehy*

I enjoy convalescence. It is the part that makes illness worthwhile.

> —*Playwright, critic, and social reformer*
> *George Bernard Shaw*

*W*e are usually the best men when in the worst health.

—*English proverb*

_____

_____

_____

_____

_____

_____

_____

_____

_____

_____

Wisdom

- The most important thing I learned about myself was . . .
- What I found most difficult to accept is . . .
- What I am most grateful for is . . .
- I gained many new insights into people and their views of sickness. They included:
- What helped me to best accept my situation and make peace with it was . . .

*M*y life has changed because I am finally facing
who I am. Who I have become.
                    —*Writer Andrea Dominick*

*I*nside myself is a place where I live all alone and that's where you renew your springs that never dry up.

—*Novelist and humanitarian Pearl S. Buck*

*I*n the depth of winter, I finally learned that within me lay an invincible summer.

> —*Philosopher, novelist, and playwright Albert Camus*

Section 4
Memories

*W*riting *About the Most Traumatic Event in Your Life*

A study in the April 1999 issue of the *Journal of the American Medical Association* concluded that patients who wrote about the most stressful event in their lives showed significant improvements in their health. In an editorial accompanying the study, Stanford University School of Medicine professor and psychiatrist David Spiegel, MD, wrote that illness may trigger associations to past traumatic events. What's more, he wrote, the way patients responded to being sick often affected the course of their illness. The questions in this section are designed to evoke responses similar to those asked for in the study's writing exercise developed by James Pennebaker, PhD, a psychologist at the University of Texas at Austin, and his colleagues.

• The most traumatic experience I've had occurred when I was _____ years old. And this is what happened . . .

_____

_____

_____

_____

- The people involved included . . .

• I reacted by . . .

- I have vivid memories of how I felt at the time . . .

• What I felt most powerless about was . . .

- What I learned from the experience was . . .

- As the years have gone by, I've made peace with what happened by . . .

- My illness or injury brought back some of the same feelings that I experienced at the time of this past event, including . . .

- Having survived this earlier trauma, I feel that I can cope with my current situation by . . .

_____

_____

_____

_____

_____

_____

_____

_____

_____

_____

Section 5
Relationships

Secrets

- The feelings I was (am) not able to share with family and friends during this time include(d) . . .
- I was first able to share my inner thoughts and fears with . . . and what I most remember about that conversation was . . .
- I first realized that my sickness or injury was making me a difficult person to get along with when . . .

Not to transmit an experience is to betray it.
—*Holocaust survivor and historian Elie Wiesel*

*T*rouble is part of your life, and if you don't share it, you don't give the person who loves you a chance to love you enough.

—*Entertainer Dinah Shore*

*T*he truth is cruel, but it can be loved and it makes free those who have loved it.

—*Philosopher, poet, and writer George Santayana*

_____

_____

_____

_____

_____

_____

_____

_____

_____

_____

*S*upport

- I was strengthened by the way these friends, colleagues, or family members supported me . . .
- What most comforted me about how others reacted to my situation was . . .
- Here are some of the good things that strengthened my relationships with others . . .

*T*his is love: to fly toward a secret sky, to cause a
hundred veils to fall each moment. First, to let
go of life. Finally, to take a step without feet.

—*Poet and mystic Rumi*

All, everything that I understand, I understand only because I love.
　　　　—*Novelist and philosopher Leo Tolstoy*

I no longer cared about survival—I merely loved.
    —*Anthropologist and author Loren Eiseley*

*C*hange

- The relationship most affected by my injury/illness was with . . . for these reasons:
- I couldn't change the impact of my health on this relationship, but I am trying to make things better in these ways . . .
- There are both positive and negatives aspects of the changes, including . . .
- When I knew that I might be able to care for myself in the future, I decided to try to change these relationships:
- I'm especially grateful for the deeper relationship I developed with this friend or relative . . . because . . .

*C*hange your life today. Don't gamble on the future,
act now, without delay.
—*Philosopher, feminist, and writer*
Simone de Beauvoir

*T*hings do not change. We do.
—*Essayist and naturalist*
Henry David Thoreau

There is a time for departure even when there's no certain place to go.

—*Playwright Tennessee Williams*

*E*xpectations

- What most disappointed me about how others reacted to my illness or accident was . . .
- I got to the point where I no longer had time or energy for people who . . .
- The imbalance or abusiveness in my relationship with . . . became apparent to me when . . .
- Here's what I resolved to do (or did) about it . . .
- I realized how important it was to mend fences with . . . at this point in my illness . . . and decided to take this action:

*D*on't compromise yourself. You are all you've got.
—*Singer Janis Joplin*

---

*H*ope is the only good thing that disillusion respects.

—*Moralist Marquis de Vauvenargues*

*I*f I die, I forgive you; if I recover, we shall see.
—*Spanish proverb*

$\mathcal{N}$ew Friends

- I found kinship and understanding with other patients through . . .
- I am inspired by people who are further along in their illness/recovery than am I in these ways . . .
- What those who share my illness/injuries can give me that friends and family cannot is . . .

_____

_____

_____

_____

_____

_____

_____

_____

_____

*T*hat's what friendship means: sharing the prejudice of experience.

—*Author Charles Bukowski*

*E*ach friend represents a world in us, a world possibly not born until they arrive, and it is only by this meeting that a new world is born.
—*Writer and critic Anaïs Nin*

*W*hen you learn to live for others, they will live for you.

—*Author Paramahansa Yogananda*

Section 6
Battling Setbacks

$\mathcal{A}$ Fighting Spirit

- When I encounter a setback, this is what happens . . .
- Here's how I fight back . . .
- The person(s) who is (are) most instrumental in my struggle against setbacks is (are) . . . because . . .
- I try to conserve my strength by . . .
- Even though I'm hurting, I find that I can act more normal if I . . .

*W*e live our lives as commuters, one month overwhelmed by the sheer gravity of a diagnosis, by the dismay of a new symptom, the next buoyed up by a new diet, a new drug, a new resolve.

—*Professor Patricia Foster*

*F*all seven times, stand up eight.

—*Japanese proverb*

_____

_____

_____

_____

_____

_____

_____

_____

_____

_____

_____

I am not afraid of storms, for I'm learning how to sail my ship.

—*Novelist Louisa May Alcott*

*Y*ou may be disappointed if you fail, but you are doomed if you don't try.
—*Opera singer and director Beverly Sills*

*P*ain and *D*iscomfort

- The most persistent pain I have had to deal with is . . .
- Here is how I learned to live with pain:
- I need medication to deal with this kind of pain:
- Pain is disruptive to my life in this way:
- I have found the best antidote to pain to be . . .

*T*he real test of a happy life is to see how much pain and loss and frustration can be endured and absorbed without spoiling the joy of it.
—*Educator and humanitarian Rufus Jones*

I have sometimes been wildly, despairingly, acutely miserable . . . but through it all I knew quite certainly that just to be alive is a grand thing.
—*Mystery writer and playwright Agatha Christie*

*L*aughter is the tonic, the relief, the surcease for pain.

—*Comedian and actor Charlie Chaplin*

Limitations

- These are the things I can do and still take great satisfaction in:
- These are the things I wish I could do that I cannot do easily or without great effort or pain:
- I am able to get around my limitations with this help or these tools:
- I have learned to accept and live with my limitations by . . .

I'm a slow walker, but I never walk back.
　　　　　　—*President Abraham Lincoln*

*Y*ou commit a sin of omission if you do not utilize all the power that is within you.

> —*Physician, professor, and writer Oliver Wendell Holmes*

*R*ecovering (from chronic illness) is similar to recovery from the devastation of a flood, for you don't know exactly when crisis begins and when it ends. The only certainty is that it will surely flood again.

—*Poet, essayist, and professor Mary Swander*

Mental Strength

- I sought solace in doing these new things:
- These books or music provided solace and inspiration to me:
- I found that this activity was the best way for me to get my mind off myself and my own problems:
- I have found the will to get through difficult periods with these routines:
- When I need inspiration to get through a day, I . . .

*F*aith moves mountains, but you have to keep pushing while you are praying.

—*Author Mason Cooley*

*C*ourage is fear holding on a minute longer.
　　　—*U. S. general and military strategist*
　　　George S. Patton

_____

_____

_____

_____

_____

_____

_____

_____

_____

_____

Alternative Treatments

- I sought out alternatives to traditional health care when . . .
- What worked best for me was . . .
- These were the difficulties I faced in seeking out alternative treatments:
- The reaction of friends and family to my seeking unconventional treatment was . . .
- The outcome of my alternative treatment was . . .

_____

_____

_____

_____

_____

_____

_____

_____

*T*hat which does not destroy me makes me stronger.

—*Philosopher and poet Friedrich Nietzsche*

*E*ven in the deepest sinking there is the hidden
purpose of an ultimate rising. Thus it is for all
men, from none is the source of light withheld
unless he himself withdraws from it. Therefore
the most important thing is not to despair.

—*Hasidic saying*

Surviving means being born over and over.
—*Writer Erica Jong*

Section 7
The Future

$\mathcal{H}$opes and Concerns

- My hopes for my future are . . .
- My hopes for my loved ones' future are . . .
- My biggest concerns about the future are . . .
- What I fear most about becoming more ill is . . .

*T*he beginning is always today.
  —*Novelist, short-story writer, and*
  feminist Mary Wollstonecraft

*N*ever think that God's delays are God's denials.
Hold on; hold fast; hold out. Patience is genius.
— *Mathematician and naturalist*
Comte de Buffon

*T*he butterfly counts not months but moments,
And has time enough.

> —*Poet, novelist, and essayist*
> *Rabindranath Tagore*

*W*ork

- I was able to continue (or resume working) on this basis:
- Keeping my hand in my work helped because . . .
- When I reflect on the work I was doing prior to my illness/ accident, I feel this way about it:
- I hope to find a different kind of work than what I was doing because . . .
- I feel this way about the idea of returning to work (volunteer or paid):
- What I most miss about being able to work is . . .

*T*he world is sown with good; but unless I turn my glad thoughts into practical living and till my own field, I cannot reap a kernel of the good.
—*Memoirist, essayist, and lecturer*
Helen Keller

*W*ork is the grand cure of all the maladies and
miseries that ever beset mankind.
—*Essayist and historian Thomas Carlyle*

*W*e work to become, not to acquire.
—*Editor, writer, and printer*
Elbert Hubbard

$\mathcal{M}$indset

- These are the ways that I think I will act differently in the future:
- My perspective on the small disappointments that turn up regularly in life is likely to change in this way:
- There are things unrelated to my illness/accident that I feel I handle with more confidence. They include:
- I hope to become more this kind of person as time goes on:
- The biggest mental battles I find myself fighting are . . .

*T*he secret of health for both mind and body is not to mourn for the past, not to worry about the future, not to anticipate troubles, but to live the present moment wisely and earnestly.

—*The Buddha*

*N*o pessimist ever discovered the secret of the stars, or sailed to an uncharted land, or opened a new discovery for the human spirit.

　　　　—*Memoirist, essayist and lecturer*
　　　　Helen Keller

*D*eep in their roots,
All flowers keep the light.
—Poet Theodore Roethke

*G*oals

- I hope to be able to spend my time doing more of these activities:
- Because of my illness/accident, I hope to be able to help others in these ways:
- These are places I've thought about going to that I hope to visit when I'm able to:
- I hope to spend more time with these people:
- I hope to be able to do these things with the people I love:
- I have found myself drastically redefining what I must do in my lifetime . . .

*T*he greatest pleasure in life is doing what people say you cannot do.

—*Social scientist and literary critic Walter Bagehot*

*T*he significance of a man is not in what he attains, but rather in what he longs to attain.

—*Poet, novelist, and painter*
Kahlil Gibran

---

*A*h, but a man's reach should exceed his grasp,
or what's a heaven for?

—*Poet Robert Browning*

_____

_____

_____

_____

_____

_____

_____

_____

_____

_____

_____

Living with Dying

- My views about death and an afterlife have changed in these ways:
- My spirituality has developed in these ways:
- What I most fear about not being alive is . . .
- What concerns me most about how my family and friends act after I'm gone is . . .
- I plan or am doing the following things so that those who depend on me will find it easier to cope in my absence:
- When my time comes, I will be ready because . . .

*B*elieve that life is worth living, and your belief
will help create the fact.
—*Philosopher William James*

_____

_____

_____

_____

_____

_____

_____

_____

_____

_____

I'll tell you a great secret, my friend. Don't wait for
the Last Judgment. It happens every day.
          —*Philosopher, novelist, and playwright*
          Albert Camus

*T*hose who live are those who fight.
　　　　—*Poet, novelist, and playwright*
　　　　Victor Hugo

_____

_____

_____

_____

_____

_____

_____

_____

_____

_____

_____

*T*here is the fear that there is an afterlife but no one will know where it's being held.
—*Film director and actor Woody Allen*

Recovery of soul and recovery of the health of the body may occur together or not; healing may occur, and the body may not survive.
—*Writer and lecturer Jean Shinoda Bolen*

_____

_____

_____

_____

_____

_____

_____

_____

_____

_____

*T*he journey is the reward.

—Taoist saying

Notes

Acknowledgments

My thanks to the following people, whose insights and suggestions were invaluable: Kathy Hoekenga, Sandra Leanza, Sherie McCaffrey, and Jim Mitchell.

The quotes used in *The Book of My Healing* came from a number of sources including:

Jean Shinoda Bolen, MD. *Close to the Bone: Life-Threatening Illness and the Search for Meaning* (Scribner's, 1996).

Robert I. Fitzhenry, ed. *The Harper Book of Quotations*, 3rd ed. (HarperCollins, 1993).

Patricia Foster and Mary Swander. *The Healing Circle: Authors Writing of Recovery* (Plume, 1998).

The Princeton Language Institute. *21st Century Dictionary of Quotations* (Dell Publishing, 1993).

Website: www.spiritsong.com/quotes

Stay in Touch . . .
Learn More

For more information and research updates on writing as a tool for healing or to contact the author, visit Peggy Schmidt's Website: http://www.writetoheal.net.

If you are interested in purchasing a copy of *The Writing to Heal Workshop Leader's Guide*, please contact the author at the Website above or by writing to her at: 30 Bear Gulch Drive, Portola Valley, California 94028.

About the Author

Peggy Schmidt is the author of five books, a magazine writer, and a newspaper columnist. She has taught feature writing at New York University, and was an editor at *Glamour* magazine for six years. She is a book producer and is the West Coast Director of the American Book Producers Association.

Also available

The Book of Myself
A Do-it-Yourself Autobiography in 201 Questions

Carl & David Marshall

0-7868-6250-5

The Book of Us
A Journal of Your Love Story in 150 Questions

David & Kate Marshall

0-7868-6477-X